The making of Dirt is Good

The making of Dirt is Good
A personal journey of Brand Transformation

David Arkwright
Former Global VP Persil and Omo, Unilever
Founder of MEAT Global Brand Consultancy

LONDON   MONTERREY
MADRID   SHANGHAI
MEXICO CITY BOGOTA
NEW YORK   BUENOS AIRES
BARCELONA SAN FRANCISCO

Published by

LID Publishing Limited
One Adam Street, London WC2N 6LE

31 West 34th Street, 8th Floor, Suite 8004,
New York, NY 10001, U.S.

info@lidpublishing.com
www.lidpublishing.com

A member of:

www.businesspublishersroundtable.com

© MEAT
© LID Publishing Ltd, 2013
Reprinted 2016

Printed in Great Britain by TJ International Ltd
ISBN: 978-1-907794-46-9
Cover design: Jenny Knowles
Page design: Jenny Knowles

For Dad

Notes and Acknowledgements

The making of Dirt is Good is strictly a personal memoir and as such does not seek to represent definitive facts or occurrences. It seeks to give only a personal retrospective on the initial creation of the brand from 2000-2005. During this period, 'Dirt is Good' was the work of many – not least the global brand team members who took part in this first stage of the journey.

Since then the brand has been successfully stewarded to ever greater success by subsequent talented teams – all of whom are respectfully saluted by this memoir.

Contents

Apocalypse

Creating a vivid definition of the brand and business challenge. In which we take a fresh look at competitiveness from a global perspective, our vulnerabilities emerge and the looming threat of a joined-up global competitor announces itself.

As we survey the wreckage of 60 years of business success, we ask ourselves where has it all gone wrong. How can it be that this vast empire of great national businesses – the brands themselves often a scene of bloody and victorious battles – can suddenly appear so vulnerable when seen as a whole? This is the scene confronting us on that early autumn day in 1998 as we find the last pieces of the jigsaw that is the global laundry business, and insert them to complete the full picture of our newly fragmented world.

We have undertaken the painstaking task of reviewing every single pack design of what purports to be the same brand globally and inserting them in their new home – the map of the world. And as this final piece of the jigsaw takes its place on this new world stage, the completed picture emerges as being uncannily incomplete.

What ought to emerge as a powerful global business, in which the whole exceeds the sum of its parts, appears as quite the opposite. For here in front of us is a business now self-evidently riddled with inconsistency and difference, as opposed to being united by commonality and integrity. In short, a business that has assumed itself to be in good health, only to be told that this most cursory of examinations reveals the need for a fresh look at what lies behind these first warning signs of disintegration.

It's curious how brands become a very real representation of what consumers are and are not; have been and have become. The relatively banal world of packaging design can be the catalyst for huge protracted debates about a country's history, its psyche and its development. A seemingly innocuous "Swoosh" or "Swirl" on a detergent pack becoming retrospectively associated with the changing state of emancipation of the post-colonial Malaysian woman. A "Starburst" design the very symbolic manifestation of the black African's strife against the repressive forces of apartheid.

The truth, of course, is that many of these designs – now imbued with such vivid symbolism – were in fact designed by a factory manager from Port Sunlight circa 1963.

More detailed examination followed. It was long and thorough. For beneath the hordes of different designs – and the apparent consumer sovereignty they portrayed – were hidden bigger themes of difference and diversity. Advertising, brand names, formulations, perfumes, ingredient specifications all emerged as fundamentally different as we moved across national borders. It felt odd that the short journey across the frontier from Singapore to Malaysia could unearth such radical differences in what some people saw as mere washing powder. Or indeed that consumers – known to most of the world as human beings – could be really so different just because they happened to carry a different passport.

But the truth was that the fragmented hotchpotch would be found to conceal more serious issues. Underlying this fragmentation lurked a business that was fundamentally ill-equipped to cope with the new joined-up world. Its historic disjointedness – once a celebration of great national conquests and still in many cases relatively successful brands and businesses – had become a disability. By smashing the world to smithereens, the business had also smothered its very competitiveness as business efficiencies fell down the cracks between the countries. Technology – for so long the means by which these brands had faced up to their aggressors – suddenly looked hopelessly lame. The differences which had been assumed from country to country had ripped the technological arsenal into very small weapons. Weapons which were now needed to hold off attack from a very strong global competitor with global scale on his side.

Invincibility had become vulnerability in the time it had taken to merely change the lens of the microscope: we were coming second in the contest for consumers' minds. Unfortunately first prize was won by a monster. A monster from Cincinnati.

Lessons

1 Create a compelling visualisation of the challenge ahead.

Finding a way of visualising the brand and business problem which confronts you is a critical step in gaining buy-in from those entrenched in previous ways of thinking.

By creating a map of the world showing the numerous different pack designs, the team was able to stimulate a business discussion about fragmentation and its consequences in terms of the bottom line. The pack designs symbolised a culture of different countries acting as separate entities. Beneath this lay obvious similar issues in terms of communication, formulations, ingredients specifications and attitudes.

We are often far too sophisticated in how we seek to communicate tough business truths. Getting the right stimulus in place is often the right way to evoke the desired response.

2 Respect the past as a way of forging the future.

By visualising the packs in this way the team was in a position to engage with the past of the brand, and those responsible for creating this history, on the basis of understanding and respect. The things that 'Brand Adventurers' need to change in the interest of progress were in most cases put in place with good reason and intent.

Engaging with the history of the brand is the best way to start to see its future – and doing so with previous inventors can only add to internal brand traction.

3 Create a detailed analysis of both brutal facts and positive truths.

Building a true picture of what we really knew, and as importantly, what we did not know was a significant basis for change. The painstaking analysis of different designs, advertising, ingredients etc was the key to seeing the potential pattern for breakthrough. Without this we would still be labouring under the sense of impossibility – the sense that the brands are all different and could never be united by a single, powerful idea which the world could believe in.

The truth – forensically derived – is the way to forge a path forward, and the way to push away the 'old think' which obscures forward movement.

4 Use newfound engagement with the new reality to radically challenge conventional wisdom.

Not only did the new perspective on the world show a position which was fundamentally at odds with a vision for a globally competitive business, it forced a re-evaluation of the internal myth that Unilever was superior in Laundry. A number 1 position in many countries dissolved into a harsh realisation of global inferiority – which was to spur a huge agenda of brand and business repair.

By creating a 'burning platform' we can rapidly open debates which challenge conventional wisdom which has prevailed for decades.

Shrink the world

Re-connecting with the consumer at a profound human level. In which we create a brand mission and begin a fundamental, and fundamentally different understanding of common consumer motivations.

The thought of taking a huge eraser and rubbing out the lines which delineate nations has had enduring appeal throughout history for more cynical politicians than those that grace the corridors of a huge multinational.

We set out to prove that these lines – apparently so firm, as evidenced by the differences in brands from country to country – were in fact written in the faintest pencil.

But we also had a hunch that what we were generously calling brands were probably in many cases no more than trademarks. Trademarks which had served great purpose over time in offering reassurance of quality and reliability. We also had a sense that these trademarks – which had for so long served as a means of separating one product from another to the consumer's advantage – had now come up against brand equity's very own flesh-eating disease – commoditisation. It seemed that the more we became locked in hopeless international debate about combating the plagiarism that threatened our brands, the more real price would sink and our brands become ever more destined for the bargain bin. We were slowly being reduced to a marketing game more concerned with aping the competition than connecting with women and families across the world as the world changed around them. The freer the world was becoming – with vistas of opportunity opening up at fantastic pace – the more this category seemed to be locking our consumers into a life of marketing drudgery.

A vision was starting to emerge in our team. We wanted to create the first truly global brand which could reconnect in a genuinely meaningful way with the millions of housewives across the world.

It wasn't as if we didn't know much. In many ways we were afforded far greater consumer understanding than our intelligence could bear. We were inundated with a plethora of habits and attitudes, statistics and data. But ironically we had become so organised – putting everything away into neatly labelled boxes – that we were no longer capable of finding what we were looking for any more.

We started by seeking to understand what was really going on in people's heads. We had for too long developed an unhealthy obsession with people's wash bowls and their stains. And this obsession had led to a behaviour that increasingly consisted of boasting about the size of our molecules. We wanted to go beyond the washbowl, put our molecules away for the moment, and focus on what really moved people.

Our plan and approach was relatively simple. We would listen to our consumers – in some 21 countries around the world – in an altogether more real way. By asking consumers the simple and persistent question in relation to their laundry "Why is that important to you?" we would seek to get beyond the banal, and into the real meaning of their lives. We would combine this free-wheeling approach with the kind of methodological fascism hitherto unknown to the company.

Our interviews were to be conducted by one research company across all six continents. The methodology and approach was non-negotiable. We would seek to see the consumer as one mind rather than one washbowl. We would use the language of questions rather than the didactic sledgehammer of assertion. In short we began to listen.

As the outcome of this started to form, we were shocked. The people we talked to would often be reduced to tears by our interrogation. But we did not beat them into submission – in fact we had interested them into re-understanding the way that what may seem at times the banal act of washing clothes would fit into the rich tapestry of their lives and ambitions. Within five questions we would free our subjects from being chained to the washbowl, to freely speaking with huge passion about their lives, their selves, their fears, their families and how all of these related to the world of washing clothes.

At the other side of the huge corporate mirror, with its language of enzymes, molecules and unstoppable superlatives, was a real human being the world over. And behind this human being hid a huge amount of passion pertaining to this category. By inverting our microscope and seeing laundry in the context of their lives – as opposed to their lives in the context of laundry – we had found a treasure-chest of possibility.

We sensed, for the first time, the lines which had separated our brands and our perceptions of the consumers beneath them starting to be erased. Our consumers had been separated by faint pencil. This was to prove the finding that propelled us into four years of major convergence, the like of which our business could never have imagined. We were to collapse this menagerie of fragmented packs, perfumes, advertising and parochial approaches into an altogether more meaningful global whole.

But as we started to erase the pencil lines, we found that the barons were to have insisted on indelible ink.

Lessons

1 Gather all the intelligence available, digest it and discard it.

We are all too often mesmerised by the heaps of data statistics and consumer information which we have available. But the truth so often is that it has become an un-usable barrier to forward thinking. We become far to overloaded for our own intelligence as marketers – and as human beings.

By taking the time to assemble the key data which has underpinned the thinking of the status quo, we gain license to do what is often the right step – to leap beyond it into a simpler, more profound understanding with which the organisation can engage.

2 Elevate the debate to a higher altitude.

Big Ideas are borne out of thinking which operates beyond statistics. Counter-intuitively, the apparent sophistication of the market research industry can lead us all too often to operate at a level which misses the point of real profound connection.

3 Understand that consumers naturally integrate functionality with meaning.

Consumers simply do not make the distinction between a brand's functionality and its emotional benefit. This distinction is in fact a confection of the marketing industry – developed to fill in boxes in Brand Keys or any other brand model. Real people experience brands as an integrated whole – what the brand does being seamlessly integrated into what the brand means in the consumer's mind. And much of this is happening at the sub-conscious level. In this case, the false separation of functional and emotional benefits had stopped the brand(s) from realising their potential to mean more.

Using research approaches which really integrate the functional and emotional meaning of the brand is the way to move away from a divisive, and ultimately unhelpful conventional way of thinking.

4 Create a simple, heartfelt and moving connection with what really matters to those that might buy your brand.

By working in one-on-one approaches with consumers, and essentially asking the same question over and over again – 'Why is that important to you?' – we were able to connect at a profound level with what really moves human beings about the category.

We are often all too locked into a brand-centric understanding of consumers – believing that consumers really care about the microscopic details of our brands. By seeing our brand in the context of the consumer's world, hopes, fears and real life, we were able to elevate ourselves into the real zone of connection.

5 Don't merely hear consumers, listen to what they say.

Asking the right questions in the right way is an important step towards creating a breakthrough understanding of the consumer – and a platform from which to effect change. Even more critical is having the courage to really listen to what the consumer is really saying.

We sometimes hear but do not listen. By asking the right questions and using daring stimulus, we were able to see a whole set of new connections which would not normally sit together. We unblocked our ears – stuffed for many years with a tiresome obsession with stains – and started to really hear how this related to the bigger picture of consumers' lives, hopes and dreams.

6 Treat the world with an unwaveringly common approach to real consumer understanding.

By insisting on a common approach to consumer understanding, and the consequence of using the same company to conduct this work, we would never gain friends amongst the barons. What we were able to gain was the first ever truly global take on the emotions which really governed our category. We also insisted that there would not be any local debriefs of findings from individual countries – despite the fact that they were to pay for the work.

7 Use the deep commonality and profundity of consumers to cut through the complexity imposed by the organisation.

Human beings share many common values and beliefs at a profound level – and as such are often far more similar than they are dissimilar.

You can use the commonality of consumers as a means of cutting through prejudices which have often been forged over generations of management.

Blurred vision

Developing a motivating vision of the future.
In which we define a common ambition and ways of working. We set about anatomising our brand in a way which exposes commonality and possibility.

Knowing the world was not the labyrinth it had at first appeared was a huge incentive to move forward. The formative brand team, in truth as unlikely a rag bag of marketing directors as the motley crew of brands they represented, started to see some possibilities. Maybe we could get to a brand which was truly global and relevant.

Our first step was to create some assumptions about the basic shape of the portfolio and the anatomy of the brands which might sit within it.

We had started to put together the beginnings of a vision. A vision which perversely had not yet an end-point and was characterised more by obscurity than by lucidity. We had vague notions of where we wanted to go and boundless ambition filling in the gaps. We realised the need to firm up this ambition and the way we would work to achieve it. We would build laundry's first $2-billion brand. We cleverly set the timeframe for this accomplishment as the beginning of the new millennium. It felt sufficiently far away for us to complete this gargantuan task.

Beneath this vision we had started to define some ways of working and thinking. We articulated amongst ourselves the desire to cast off our regional and functional identities and work with each other as imagined global brand entrepreneurs. We organised ourselves at this very early stage as a global brand board and insisted, as any good board would, on the right support. We appointed a Financial Director for our brand board. We assumed a Chairman. We had a mission. We had strategic thrusts. More critically, we had created a bubble within the business that we tried to keep slightly outside of the business' sight. We had started to set ourselves aside from the day-to-day current of the business.

And within our bubble we agreed some ways in which we would work – one of which we called 'A Vivid Brand World'. We insisted that at every meeting of our board we should analyse and understand at least one brand we admired. We

29

figured that by emulating what we considered to be great brands we might learn to dissipate our own inertia in the laundry category. We also figured there was a great distance between positive emulation and the mindless plagiarism we had fallen into the habit of in recent years. We banned our immediate competition from the room and were to maintain this draconian discipline for the next three years. Anyone fascinated with P&G – or what we called suffering from 'P&Gness envy' – had no right to be on our journey.

From the banal world of plagiarised molecules we were soon to find ourselves in the vivid brand world of what we saw as truly great brands. Month after month we studied the likes of Apple, Volvo, Levi's, Nike, then latterly the fashion brands of Gucci, Chanel, Prada and beyond. We refused to believe that great marketing was the preserve of the elite brands. Instead we saw it as the privilege of our consumers – no matter how seemingly banal the category or where they happened to live.

Deep in the bowels of Corporate HQ a small team was set to work on the most unforgiving of tasks. Armed with reels of TV ads from around the world, brand positioning statements, hundreds of press ads and any other fragments of information which could be gleaned from the annals of the brands' histories, the team poured through this vast array of material in search of patterns and possible anatomies of these brands. The Laddering Study had told us that consumers' minds, imagination and values were more similar than their passports would suggest. We now set out to unearth the brand ideologies which lay fossilised beneath the debris of years of often undistinguished advertising and hollow claims.

It was from the bowels of the building that the aptly named 'Bog Roll' was to emerge. A long, thin roll of paper, detailing what we perceived to be the founding ideologies of each of the different brand positionings. With huge rigour we picked out the functional and emotional promises of the emerging brand shapes: their personalities, their values, their key depictions and language over the years. We sat them side-by-side in order to highlight the differences across the brands and to define the coherence and integrity within each of the brand shapes.

This seminal piece of paper came to symbolise for the team a new beginning. The Bog Roll was used to wipe away years of obfuscation which had enveloped these brands over time. And in doing so we were to find some basic brand anatomies which not only appeared to have real internal consistency, but appeared rooted in a set of values and foundational beliefs which might well prove pertinent going forward.

We had stripped back the brands to the set of ideas and beliefs which they appeared to truly represent. Behind each of the brand anatomies we had started to picture a very real human being defined and described by her view of the world, her family, her life and how all of these might just pertain to laundry. She was no longer defined by nationality but rather united in an ever more vivid picture of real life the world over.

We then began to rebuild a 'bionic' brand from the various pieces of film which we felt epitomised the brand's characteristics. We set out 'bionic outlines' of each of the brands we thought might sit in the portfolio, getting a sense of their functional beliefs and their purpose in existing as a whole. We then had the satisfaction of seeing the Bog Roll brought to life in steelomatic form, and comparing these with the models of inconsistency which many of our national laundry brands had slipped into over time. This villainous tape – which compared what we had become to what lay beneath the years of gradual deviation and inconsistency – was to become a critical tool in convincing the barons of the need to move forward. The evidence of the problem was incontrovertible.

We became more and more acquainted with what these brands had stood for and could stand for. When stripped back to their foundational beliefs, they seemed to embody a coherent integrity of purpose, ambition and functionality. Indeed they were Top Performance and indeed they were top performers – but they were also acquainted with the human lives in which they played a part. We started to see the complicity that many of these brands had struck up with 1960s housewives around the world. This was as evident in the black and white world of Persil Great Britain as it was in the paddy fields of Breeze Thailand's evolution and the streets of Sao Paulo where Omo had gained celebrity.

We had found the core of our brands and had started to realise that maybe it could be re-imbued with the sense of purpose which underpinned the likes of Apple and Nike – which we admired so much.

It was at this time that another ideological and scatological truth began to emerge. 'There is no such thing as a shitty category; there is just shitty brand management!' And to prove this we went one step further. Having enjoyed different speakers at each brand board, from such diverse brands as Action Man and Skoda, we went for the ultimate test of our new ethos. Fresh from 15 years in the toilet paper industry, we invited the unlikely brand consultant who had built Kimberly Clark's Andrex brand into one of the most loved and compelling brands in the supermarket. We were sure that even the most basic functionality in a brand needed presenting with relevant imagination and emotional integration.

We began to walk the brand positioning anatomies around the world, slowly starting to gain some sympathy from the barons for the task at hand.

And we now had the permission to nail our assumptions one step further in what became the biggest laundry quantitative study ever. We spoke to some 21,000 consumers in more than 20 countries. Our aim was to check out whether our assumptions, as hypothesised in the Bog Roll, were indeed true in the market-place. And whether – all things being equal – consumers related to the respective brands in their markets in much the same way the world over. Despite a conviction within the brand board that 'You don't make sheep any fatter by weighing them', we knew nonetheless the importance of solidifying our assumptions with numbers. And we also knew that more than ever we would need more rigour in ensuring a common approach to this quantification. Tautologous as it may seem, if you ask people different questions you will get different answers. We could not afford different answers.

But the killer punch was convincing each region to pay for their percentage of the research quantification. We needed a united approach to this work and any problems which may emerge had to be problems shared.

And as the scatological theme continued one step further any requests for financial assistance were rebutted. As the then Global Leader would retort to any complainants: 'It's no good shitting on your own doorstep then ringing the bell to ask for paper'!

Lessons

1 Articulate a bold vision for the brand which has the power to change perceptions of the task at hand – however obscure the route to the destination may be.

We were quick to lay down an audacious goal for the business – despite at this point not being too sure if or how the destination would be achieved. The start point for this was to define a clear destination point for the brand – in this case to build a $2-billion global brand. The critical point here was to use a language – that of hard dollars – which could easily make the business sit up and notice that we meant business. The sheer size of the numbers when seen as a joined up brand business could not help but feel attractive to anyone in the business – due to the scale it promised and the new potential competitiveness this would therefore bring about.

2 Every brand can be great, and every company can have great brands.

We developed a mindset which refused the standard 'low self-esteem' marketing which can surround everyday brands. By assuming a start point which says that there is nothing that disqualifies such an apparently banal category from being supremely interesting, and from our brand from leading this, we opened our minds to possibility. It is all too easy for brands to assume self-limiting approaches to brand development. By externalising our thinking and by analysing other brands, we were to realise that the great brands we so admired had in effect chosen to make categories which hitherto had been uninteresting, appear engaging. This is the power of ideas – and the ambition to realise them.

3 Assume a team identity which is empowering and motivating.

Big breakthrough ideas are borne of teams of people who feel that they have the license to make real change happen. They are borne out of a sense of self-determination and a sense of authority to drive change. Unfortunately this authority is rarely readily available to brand teams – of course depending on the stage of development of the global organisation. In this case we assumed this identity, as opposed to asking for permission. We became a self-appointed Brand Board – with all of the requisite board functions in place. This had a critical role in creating a sense of heroic mission – and the critical sense of belonging which good teams need.

4 Define bold strategic thrusts which can really guide an agenda of change en route to the destination.

By laying down an agenda of change, we could start to see the broad pathway to the destination – and could start to designate who would do what in service of creating a $2-billion brand. Amongst the five strategic thrusts were the need to create a true brand which truly connects; commit to a constant external orientation for the brand and brand team in order to learn and grow, resulting in a vivid brand world in which we would live; and build joint approaches to innovation which maximised scale and drove brand uniqueness.

5 Build a vivid brand world via positive emulation of outside brands.

In driving an agenda of change it was very important to ensure that the insularity which engulfed thinking was actively and systematically challenged. We started to build this new mindset by insisting that in every meeting there would be real and relevant inspiration from external brands which were making change in the world. The team spent far more time analysing Nike, Apple, Gucci, Prada and Levi's and the great brand activation that was Live Aid than it did studying P&G advertising. We refused to believe that great marketing was the preserve of the so called 'elite' brands.

6 Undergo a thorough 'Brand Excavation' to define the 'Core Brand Ideology'.

By meticulously working back through the brand history we were slowly but surely equipped with a new clarity on the essential ideology which the brand had embraced in its many manifestations across different eras and countries. This not only allowed the team to understand the *fil rouge* which ran through the brand, but also the connective tissue which would see the brand into the future. Using this information to then lay down a 'Bionic Positioning'– a collage of what the best of the brand could be – allowed the team to create a sensible and solid backdrop from which to create the future.

7 Uses the 'Core Brand Ideology' to drive buy-in to a new point of departure.

When we are entrenched in the practise of the brand – and indeed the different ways the brand has been practised across time and geographies – we can become defensive. Yet drilling down to a level of brand ideology unlocks a more unifying understanding of the brand. It unites the team at a level of principle which everyone can recognise and of which all can be proud. As such we recognise the past to create a point of departure into the future.

Outside in

Creating a state of formal disruption and 'macroscopic' thinking. In which we start to think about brand ideas and how they work, then go on to create potential big ideas to be explored in assertive, common global qualitative research.

By creating a sense of space and 'apartness' from the organisation at large, the spirit of entrepreneurship would start to flourish in the team. No longer did it feel quite so tied to the history of these brands – however successful they were or had been in the past. Rather, it began to feel the burning urge to resist. Not resistance for the sake of it, but resistance against the conventions and accepted wisdom that had created the status quo it so wanted to disrupt.

We had been deeply captivated by our external brand world, and had glimpsed the freedom that so many of the brands we loved seemed to offer.

We had started to understand that the brands that seemed to stand for something that appealed to us as a team were founded somehow on resolving an antagonism.

Apple had resolved the antagonism which it sensed existed between the sterile world of computers and the vibrant world of creativity. Nike had made sport and its apparel the greatest democracy ever – breaking away from the elite and bringing its chic performance ethic to the urban masses. Levi's had brought danger and rebellion into the seemingly safe world of middle class America through its jeans.

In short, all of the brands we loved offered liberation from some kind of captivity or repression. But of course, one man's freedom is another man's captivity. It was all a matter of perspective. A matter of seeing the conventions of a category with the eyes of an outsider. Painstakingly understanding its conventions in order to ruthlessly smash them to pieces.

And as this fervour started to rise, we realised that our aim was to smash our competitor. Not to copy him. In fact he was no longer our competitor – he had become our enemy. And as we would remark, 'You play tennis with a competitor. You kill an enemy.'

But the team would not allow this fervour to descend into mindless anarchy or vandalism. It had already started to accumulate a lot of knowledge from the brand anatomisation experience and the laddering which had followed. And now it had quantitative data which showed how the brands actually mapped in consumers' minds. Alarmingly it also showed that relatively poor levels of differentiation had crept in between brands – even where our brands were deemed successful.

The team had located a broad terrain in which to mine for insight. We were taken by Ogilvy's approach: 'We prefer the discipline of knowledge to the anarchy of ignorance. We pursue knowledge the way a pig pursues truffles. A blind pig can sometimes find truffles, but it helps if they know that they grow in oak forest'.

We had found the forest. The next job was to find the truffling team. And the pig.

Business sometimes seems to put an inordinate amount of trust in its executives and woefully little in anyone not on the payroll. In other words, a lot of effort is put into maintaining a culture, its norms, its beliefs, whilst natural forces of resistance reject any impostor who might disrupt it. This was to be a paradox which would trouble the team at many points along the way. The question continually posed was how to institute disruption within the team and its thinking, without the disruptive forces becoming so institutionalised that they merge into the status quo. Be it in advertising, research, design or whatever, we had to find a way of remaining dangerous, whilst appearing acceptable to the forces that be.

It was about creating a state of *formal disruption.*

Aware that an insight of sufficient disruption to overturn not just a global competitor of note but also five decades of conventional wisdom would not simply announce itself, we began to think long and hard about the insight challenge ahead and the appropriate team to lead it. We knew for sure consumers were getting what they asked for, but were not at all sure that it was what they really wanted. And we knew that we would need to intuit and delve way beyond the level of consciousness that the consumer herself could articulate and somehow access the dreams, fears and concerns which formed her life view, and within that her view of laundry.

Laddering had made her cry. We now had to locate the tear duct and understand how to stimulate it in a much more precise way the world over.

We began to recruit the team who would conduct the insight mining, confident that the best truffling pigs would probably not exist within the sanitised confines of the organisation. We armed ourselves with misfits and freaks: dissidents from the world of advertising; sociologists and psychologists; and bizarre creative people. We spent days listening to external trends and sought to understand how they might affect behaviours in our consumers across the world. For more than two months the team would trawl the world, the internet and its mind for the thoughts, connections and tensions which might prove stimulating to the consumer out there.

Seven territories began to emerge – all quite different – but underlying each was a particular take on the psyche and the values of the consumer we imagined lurked beneath. We would explore the 'Pleasure of Clean' – essentially a world of connectedness and familial warmth – all brought to life by the sense of security that pristine clean laundry conveyed.

We would enter into the obsessive world of the 'Neat Freaks', exploring the values and the self image which hid behind this kind of behaviour and the Howard Hughes types it spawned.

We sought to really understand what total delegation felt like and how modern working women really related to their growing dislocation from the chores which had so formed the generations that had gone before them. We wanted to go way beyond the ludicrous cliché of the busy working mum juggling sport, sexiness and professionalism interlaced with 'devil may care' glasses of dry white wine.

We would also look at the ultimate functional promises

which a washing powder might make in the future. Having spent days seeking to decipher what was really going on in the laboratories of the company, we set about wondering how this could really translate into something the consumer might actually want. In 'Intelligent' we spoke of laser-like targeting of stains. In 'Health' we played to what we thought was an increasing fear of infection and epidemics, with laundry the first barrier of protection for the people within.

It was the sixth area which seemed to cause us most trouble. We had seen small glimpses of a world which we instinctively found interesting. It had been seen in pockets of the world as diverse as India, Eastern Europe and North America but always in a fragmented and partial form. It was a territory which depicted the maternal relationship with children and the role children played within that. We were very aware that this was an area which had become very familiar in its sugar-sweet depictions over the decades. But we persevered, for it seemed somehow at odds with the other areas which we were exploring. It seemed to bring with it a sense of balance which was intuitively interesting when compared to the hysteria of many of the brand concepts which had gone before. Rather than focussing on the obvious benefits of cleanness, it went beyond into the broader benefits of a liberal style of parenting.

As the territories became firmer, so too did the way we began to see them visually in our minds. We had been slowly assembling a very rich collage of each of these worlds, ripping articles from magazines and stealing visual references from wherever possible. As we put all of this together we realised that we had gone way beyond conventional research stimuli and had moved into what was already a creative kind of depiction. In short, we had created stimulus that might actually stimulate a real response in consumers.

We were to show Picasso as a young boy, accompanied by a question which asked respondents to imagine what his life might have been like had he not had the freedom to experiment with his early artistic talents. We would show flower power-era children with accompanying copy asserting that only free-spirited children are happy children. We would depict young engineers, filthy dirty but absorbed in the creation of the greatest feat of engineering. We were creating a stimulating world and asserting it through the research to consumers.

It seemed that sometimes you have got to imagine the egg before you lay the chicken!

We were reaching way beyond the simplistic questions so often used to merely scratch at the surface of consumers' lives. We had created a universal pictorial language which we hoped would unlock the sub-conscious via semiotic codes. Within each territory we would surround the core thought with what we called 'trigger statements' – pithy visuals and statements which would drive the extremes of the core idea or, indeed, its limitations.

As we gathered to see the findings from the insight mining, a measure of excitement and anger filled the room. Our rigour had become ever more hard-lined in the way we managed the fieldwork. Our habit of ensuring central accountability for all consumers the world over had meant one person literally flying across six continents to brief and attend the high majority of the groups.

We had looked long and hard for the kind of researcher who could combine his own imagination and flair with the demands of international sensitivity. He would need more than a touch of the feminine. We had insisted on absolutely one debrief and one debrief only – and this was to be a global debrief in front of the whole brand board.

The findings had more than exceeded our expectations. We had started to see uncannily similar reactions to the stimulus the world over. Regardless of the 'stage of development' or 'sophistication' of our consumers, we were seeing similar results emerging around the same territories and specific pieces of stimulus whether in the back streets of Bombay, the boulevards of Paris or the favelas of Brazil. Consumers could absolutely relate to the desire to give their children a better – for which they read *freer* – upbringing. Our highly visual depiction of a child pushing another in an ingeniously cobbled together go-cart made of junk released a common spectrum of emotion the world over. The caption 'great engineers start young' would motivate the most economically aspiring Indian as much as the yearning of a cynical European for a simpler, more innocent, more optimistic world.

As the groups had proceeded, the core thought had been modified to read in full: 'If you don't let your kids get dirty, they won't grow up to be well rounded and successful adults. If you do let your kids get dirty, you will need a powder that can cope'.

Picasso – depicted via a black and white photo of him painting on a huge transparent canvas – had real resonance regardless of a nation's intimacy with modern impressionist art.

We were finding that the spirit of Picasso, freely painting and oblivious to getting dirty, was of universal appeal from South Africa to Sao Paulo. It was maybe a sign of the times that the consumers in suburban Surbiton UK were perplexed at what they deciphered as 'that bald bloke vandalising a shop front'.

We were to go back to consumers with the aim of refining this thinking. Again we went global. Again we applied the methodology and rigour that had come to characterise our approach and irritate everyone else. The second round of qualitative work came back as positive as the first but with an ever-increasing depth of understanding of how this 'free parenting' idea was working.

It seemed that within this idea was the huge promise of freedom and emancipation. Emancipation no longer just from the chore of laundry but rather in reconciling the internal conflict between authority and permissiveness that troubled mothers the world over as they sought to bring up their children as better, more free and implicitly more creative, successful human beings.

The idea seemed to re-position detergents in a broader, more contemporary arena. We were talking to the complete human being as opposed to the housewife or, worse still, the washer-woman.

By depicting a very positive world of optimism, success and happiness, facilitated by a new, more intuitive idea of being free to get dirty, we were tapping into a huge, untapped arena. The more we tightened the tourniquet, the more we exposed the veins of opportunity. We could see the world no longer as a repressive, dreary place – as had been the norm in detergents marketing – but rather as a place of promise, optimism and creativity. And all of this promise would be brought about by the power of dirt. We needed to create a brand which could insert itself into this vein.

The obsessively clean world of washing powder was slowly being overtaken by a world in which dirt would play a heroic central role.

Dirt is good. The paradox had started to make itself known.

Lessons

1 Locate the brand's point of liberty.

The really great brands that we believe in resolve
something for their consumers. In some way they set
them free – by either connecting with a deep-seated
desire, or by resolving a real tension. They 'repair
the tear' in the fabric of society. Nike offers a world
of possibility and accomplishment to many who
aspire to that – made real by the ritual of performing
in its sporting apparel. Apple offers freedom in an
information technology world which had been defined
by geekish captivity.

In our unconventional approach to insight mining,
we were looking for both a sense of the positive future
which we could associate with our consumer through
our take on laundry, whilst also seeking to understand
the 'away from' energy – the things we could push
against in order to create dynamism at the heart of the
brand's idea.

2 Avoid competitor envy at all costs.

We refused to obsess about the principal competitor
– P&G – instead choosing to pursue our own agenda
thinking. Liberating our thinking to focus on what our
brand could be, as opposed to aping the competition,
was at the core of the creation of the idea. It was an
end to 'P&Gness envy'!

3 Locate the brand terrain, and then sharpen using creative stimulus.

We created seven terrains which we felt were playing to the essential motivations that the laddering study had unlocked. We then used truly engaging, rich stimulus to really mine within these terrains.

Critical to this approach was the extent to which the 'trigger' stimulus would verge into being almost small fragments of advertising. This was the point – the more engaging we could be with the stimulus, the more we could truly excavate the beginnings of an insight and an idea with meaning.

4 Create a state of formal disruption.

By building a team of specialists, oddballs and culturally non-standard people, we were actively trying to institute a state of formal disruption. It was by constituting the team in this way that we were to find the inspiration to do things differently – to refute much of the conventional wisdom which had formed the last 50 years of the brands' histories across the world. We wanted to respect this rich history, and disrupt it at the same time.

5 Operate with central accountability, and local responsibility.

By committing together to common research across the world, we had already expressed a belief that a single global idea was possible. This informs how the research is conducted, and how the team would respond to the findings. Critical, though, is that each region has its own local responsibility for understanding what this learning means at a regional level.

6 Find the deep point of difference and express this fully.

We started to glimpse that a world of optimism, of freedom and of possibility was a possible context for the brand. We were also keen to realise that this was in many ways at odds with the principal competitor's view of the world – instead seeing laundry as a place of dutifulness, discipline and to some extent dreariness. We saw the potential for the fledgling idea to operate in a diametrically opposed way – and exploited this to the brand's advantage.

Flock

Creating a team
of committed
co-conspirators,
and dealing with
regional barons.
In which the first ever
global brief leads to
the first ever globally
relevant manifestation
of our brand idea, and
the true insight it
revealed.

How could it be that we were 15 years late, yet two years too early all at the same time? This was the paradox that started to confront us on that May day as we descended on the beautifully serene poussada, nestling deep in the Portuguese hills. The pastoral calm was interrupted only by the gentle clanking of the bells around the sheeps' necks as they scurried up the hillside. This sacred former monastery was to be the setting for our very own congregation of converts to our own big idea. But as the meeting was to unfold we would find some infidels in our midst.

We appeared to have finally seduced 60 years of difference into the potential unity of a single big idea, only to find it was the wrong time in the company's cycle to conceive. Consumers had told us that the world was ready for our new perspective on parenting and dirt. Regional operational reality was to have a different view.

With a huge sense of urgency we had taken consumers at their word, striving to capture the huge consumer responsiveness to the insight mining in the setting of a brand idea. Fresh from the field we would push the libertarian thinking which was becoming known as 'Modern Parenting' into the safe confines of a positioning tool – the Brand Key.

We had glimpsed what had instinctively felt like an extremely precious insight glistening in front of us like a diamond. We felt sure that the tension between the desire to be progressive and the need to control was important. Children and their getting dirty was sandwiched between the two. We would coin this in a longhand that would appear clumsy in hindsight: 'Getting dirty is all part of the learning necessary to become a well-rounded and successful adult'. At the very centre of the brand we had the three words 'unleashing human potential' as its essential organising principle. It seemed a long way from the 'bigger', 'better' and 'faster' superlatives of the world we were leaving behind.

But like diamonds, insights have many faces, many of

which remain hidden by the dirt that covers them. It's only by constant polishing that we might just catch the true splendour of the thought as it casts its light on all that surrounds it, making its space look momentarily but fundamentally different.

We knew we had by no means uncovered every single one of the multi-faceted dimensions of the insight, but nonetheless felt the urgency to proceed. There was a limit to how much longer we could sit around trying to chisel the diamond-like thought into ever more perfect shape. It was time now to commit to manifestations and action, reversing the temptation to hide behind the inertia of incompleteness. 'That's all very well in practice, but how does it work in theory?' would not be allowed to sap our urge to act.

As we reviewed the first ever global advertising brief, we had a sense we were somehow cheating all the years of division that so many of the briefs that preceded it had ingrained. It felt both easy and difficult all at once. We were asking our creative teams to illustrate in new and engaging ways how the very tension of freedom versus restriction, seen through the prism of getting clothes dirty, might be manifested. Nowhere to be seen was any reference to molecules or technology.

Within six weeks of the brief being issued we were to see the first ever global advertising idea for 'Modern Parenting'. Within six further weeks we were to watch, with huge trepidation, as the first rendition of the idea was seen committed to film. As opposed to proving in any way dilutive, the congregation of 28 creative teams behind one brief would prove a potent force. The work was stunning.

'No stains. No learning' was born. It featured children taking part in various learning experiences and getting dirty in the process. Ranging from painting to building the most ingenious of go-carts out of junk, we were to see the true strength of the idea brought to life. It was only through getting dirty that the children had achieved – however modest the achievement might be.

In 'Painter' the voiceover would ask mothers in four continents as they looked over their budding young Picassos 'to imagine there were no stains…' the consequences of which being that the brilliant masterpiece would also disappear. At the very heart of the idea was a simple and arresting executional idea. By creating the effect of a 'fast rewind', we would demonstrate with chilling simplicity that if there had been no stains, then the painting would also have been 'uncreated'.

As time went on 'No stains. No learning' was to spawn many different executions within the same idea, all pulled together by the pointed dilemma posed by the rewind sequence. It was an idea which was endlessly capable of local touch and colour whilst remaining resolutely one and the same idea the world over.

All good ideas remain just ideas unless they are truly embraced and brought to life in the vernacular of the brand for whom they speak and the people with whom it is connecting. We were looking for a brave pioneer to lead this thinking in the real heart of the marketplace, going beyond just TV advertising alone. We wanted to portray a philosophy of life rather than merely make a marketing campaign.

Brazil was no ordinary place to make this greatest of discontinuities happen. In what was possibly the bravest of marketing moves the category had seen, the monolithic Omo brand, fortified in consumers' minds by the five years of functional reinvention which preceded it, was to pioneer the 'Modern Parenting' approach. But neither was this an ordinary time.

The fiery breath of the Cincinnati monster breathed ever more hot on the Brazilian business' neck. This most formidable global competitor was finally declaring war on the citadel of South Latin America. He would strike at what he saw as the very heart of the Omo brand's functionality. He would promise real liberation for Latin American housewives from the chores and servitude of laundry. He would seek to position Omo as the mumsy, good for nothing of an era gone by. He was to tell the age-old story of superlative performance with the finesse and poise of an elephant trying to do ballet lessons. But unfortunately with the elephantine budgets that a competitor with a decade of better margins can muster.

The Latin American business would not be attacked in this way. Rather we were to outwit him by shifting the debate to the real tensions which we had started to understand were engulfing the Latin American housewife. The tensions between progressiveness and future promise for one's children versus restrictiveness and drudgery. We had moved the benefits way beyond the promise of clean clothes. Instead we would offer a better existence for generations to come.

But the idea was not to exist in the medium of television alone. Every aspect of the business would now rally behind the 'Modern Parenting' idea, backing it with the biggest brand activation programme ever seen. The children of Chile, Central America and Brazil would paint in the name of 'the freedom to get dirty' and the Omo brand, proving in real time the validity of the insight.

As opposed to being positioned as the mumsy, good for nothing of history, we were seeing the brand grow by 4% market share in the face of the biggest onslaught ever from the most formidable competitor.

As the body of advertising began to grow, so too did the clamour to test it in order to prove the effectiveness of the work with numerical fact.

Within six months of the brief, the 'No stains. No learning' idea had graced the television screens of four continents, with activation programmes to boot. The number junkies would not be denied their gleeful fix. Not only had 'Modern Parenting' scored better than any work that had gone before within the category, it also outscored the 'beautiful brands' which the company had so revered. The ugly category was becoming beautiful.

As time went by and the 'Modern Parenting' idea grew more and more in consumers' minds, so too did their positive outtake of the brand's credentials across a whole host of attributes. Tracking studies were to show that in Brazil the Omo brand was seen to have not only significantly improved its cleaning performance, but also to be a more modern brand than any of the competitors, Ariel and Tide included. Our 60-year-old brand was seen by consumers as more modern than the year old arrivistes from Cincinnati who were positioning themselves on their very modernity.

But having cracked the seemingly impossible, we would now be confronted by the immovable. Having shown the possibility of converging the whole fragmented world behind one idea we were to find that the very idea of convergence was dissonant with a huge swathe of the organisation.

The libertarian attitude that consumers so wanted us to express was to be muted by the conservative authorities within the business. The indelible ink had spilled further than we thought.

The hallowed peace of the monastery was to be filled with discord and unrest. The rationalists could no longer be satiated with a diet of incontrovertible fact or shepherded into the free world of 'Modern Parenting'.

As the sheep ran down the hillside their bells clanged with the most unholy din.

Lessons

1 Capture the core idea as an outline draft brand – even if more is unknown than is known.

It is only when you go through the act of assembling the brand model – in this case the Brand Key – that you start to see both the gaps and the glimpses of opportunity that the fledgling idea has in store.

By starting to do this, we were to see that the 'Modern Parenting' idea was all about 'unleashing human potential' as opposed to merely cleaning clothes. This was to prove an important breakthrough.

2 Consumers often move more quickly than brand teams do.

Despite a growing body of evidence that was saying that the 'Modern Parenting' idea was connecting very profoundly with consumers across the world, there remained significant reluctance to adopt the idea in some regions.

3 The power of assumptiveness.

By proclaiming that dirt is a good thing, consumers would take out that the brand cleaned better. It is this assumptiveness which lies at the heart of so many good ideas. They connect at a level of sub-conscious – and by stimulating a connection with this sub-conscious, the brand creates a powerful loop. Hence there is no need to tell consumers that the brand works well; this is what they delight in taking out themselves.

4 The power of joined-up creativity and the global brief.

We assumed a joined-up approach to creative development way ahead of the full organisation having got behind the emerging 'Dirt is Good' idea. By joining forces in this way – and creating a process by which to do so whilst ensuring a high common denominator approach – we were to see more new and engaging ideas in three weeks than the world had seen in years. It was this internal commitment to a common creative solution from the outset which led to 'Dirt is Good' becoming a global reality – similarly executed across every continent.

Blindness

Manifesting the brand idea with unique and compelling symbols. In which we wrestle with the challenge of creating a true brand identity which really manifests the brand's meaning – both visually and olfactively.

All around was total pitch black. Not the half darkness that allows you to pick out shapes and patterns in the still of night – but an absolute and utter darkness. Voices took on a crystal sharpness as they resonated across a room no longer blurred with the cacophony of noise of everyday life. The sense of smell was heightened to such a level that what would on any normal day prove innocuous and bland would assault the nostrils like a sword laced with camphor.

But, curiously, the total darkness of this Geneva evening would strangely serve to highlight the sharpness and distinctiveness of the team's characters, like a laser cutting through the night. A voice from the blackness from another table would immediately and automatically conjure up pictures of the person from whom it emanated, depicting them in brilliant technicolour detail.

We had created a different kind of dinner experience. We wanted to feel again how the senses really worked – and figured that by removing sight we would get closer to the other four.

Sitting in this totally black room – hosted by the blind people of Geneva – we were to have the most revelatory of evenings. We wanted to explore the real meaning of identity and the way it impacted those it came into contact with. Furthermore we wanted to understand with much more clarity how different sensory stimulus could create identity.

It was an evening of huge enjoyment and learning. Miscued slurps of wine would land in laps, only to join whole starters which had somehow escaped the guests' plates. Getting dirty was very much part of the proceedings. It just happened not to be visual. A sudden groping for something or someone to hold onto en route to the bathroom would result in significant embarrassment. Darkness made it a two-handed affair.

We had started to understand the real power of the senses.

Direct, provocative, immediate. Tough to fool. Even tougher to override. The senses speak to the mind in the language of emotions, not words. Emotions alert us to how important the findings of our senses are, not only to our well-being, but to our very survival. The senses are the fast track to human emotions.

The next day we began to work on our learnings in earnest. We wanted to translate our experiences into the new world of identity and how it might work for 'Dirt is Good'.

For some time we had admired so many brands from the outside world for their distinctiveness of approach. We had noticed that they had constructed their distinctiveness by provoking more than just a single sense. With 'Dirt is Good' we would try to emulate this distinctiveness across as many of the senses as we could arouse.

We had looked at many great brands. From Nike to Apple. From Gucci to Levi's. From Mercedes to Volvo. The Nike 'swoosh' had become imbued with the very essence of 'just do it' over time. The sonic cue of solid, Teutonic engineering had become appropriated by BMW's clicking of the car door. Apple had taken a visual depiction of the eponymous fruit and had made it synonymous with the Mac and all that it stood for. In fact all of these brands had somehow managed to take a huge and often intangible thought and manifest it into something almost palpable.

We would now set about creating this kind of identity for our 'Dirt is Good' brand. The task was to somehow capture the spirit and values of freedom and creativity whilst conjuring up visceral associations to laundry and the removal of bad dirt.

But our evening had also made us think more about our 'olfactive identity'. Surely it could not be the case that our brands could symbolise so much but be fragranced differently country to country with simply no reference to the brand's discriminating thought and offering of 'freedom to get dirty'. Our heightened sense of smell during the dinner had helped us to realise how persistently under-used this sense had become in our brand's total communication of its 'Dirt is Good' idea.

Some six months later we saw for the first time the immaculate conception of the 'Dirt is Good' identity. The 'Splat' had been born. The very embodiment of the antagonism at the heart of the brand idea, it was both beautiful and at once somehow a stain. Immediately embraced by the team, it would soon begin to sharpen the way we were to think about the brand across every aspect of its manifestation and identity.

Our world had become the 'Splatworld' – a world in which people believed in the freedom to get dirty and the values this entailed. A world which understood with profound humanity the importance of getting dirty, as much as the need to get things ready to get dirty again by cleaning brilliantly!

A world that by its very name would ring the changes with the world of the competitor we wanted to smash rather than emulate. This was our world and our agenda. The identity and its impact on the team would surely have a similar impact on the consumers it needed to engage and thrill.

It would be another year of development before 'Splatscent' was to emerge. Such was our imagination that we had now taken this away from being the sole responsibility of the beard and sandal wearing technical tribe. We now wanted them to work with the greatest of the fine fragrance divas. The lady who had learned at the knee of Estee Lauder would now be deployed to build a brand-conceived fragrance for 'Dirt is Good'. 'Splatscent' was to be born.

We had created a verbal and a visual lens for our brand through which to manifest all future thinking. We were to add to this our very own smell.

From desperate fumbling in the darkness we had begun to see the first chinks of resplendent light.

Lessons

1 Manifest the brand in a powerful symbol.

By creating the 'Splat', we were to create a semiotic short hand which would express the 'Dirt is Good' idea in an instant – regardless of geography or cultural background. Not only would this identity start to unite all of the different physical manifestations of the brand across the world, it would also become an important internal symbol of identity.

2 Conceiving of the brand through all the senses.

We found that the 'Dirt is Good' idea could be expressed across all the senses – not least that of smell. Again, by creating a common, single olfactive identity for the brand with 'Splatscent', we were to add yet another dimension of brand conceived identity that was uniquely our own.

Beach

Realising the creative essence of the brand via a virtuoso performance. In which we finally create the 'immaculate conception' of the brand via a process of draconian creative rigour.

As we glimpsed the blue of the sea beyond the mountains for the first time, that curious feeling of excitement, anticipation and mild anxiety filled our hearts. It was the feeling experienced in one's youth that somehow remains as exciting and exhilarating in all the years that follow. The timeless emotion of joy and freedom that a long journey to a seaside vacation can bring, becoming ever more intense with each sighting of the glistening blue sea, framed on only one side by a golden band of sand.

And as we finally entered the southern reaches of the Rio coastline and the salty tang of sea air filled our noses, we knew we had arrived. It had been a long and circuitous journey, through rough and unforgiving terrain. But the path we had followed along the way would now start to dissolve into the freedom of the beach.

This was to be the scene of 'Dirt is Good's' coming of age. Here we would commit to celluloid the very essence of the idea. It was in this most natural of settings that we would see children in their most primeval habitat, running wild and free.

We were to depict them working as a team with the natural and purposeful manner that totally absorbs children when they are both free and captivated. Gathering driftwood and seaweed; wrestling with the natural waves of the water; creating gulleys through which water would cascade; digging in the sand – we were to see how getting dirty had resulted in a remarkable achievement.

As the camera slowly pulled back to reveal an aerial view of a huge whale, the children's real achievement would become clear. In this minute-long epic we had captured the very essence of the 'Dirt is Good' idea.

It was a story which tapped into a timeless mystical idyll, connecting with generations past, present and future who saw symbolised in these children the true spirit of innocence, freedom and hope. As the voiceover would say: "What others see as children creating a mess, we see as children creating.

Omo believes dirt is good".

We had finally done it. We had finally declared ideological war on the confines of this particular corner of the supermarket and the heartland of our competitors. And we had captured such tension in those three words.

Perhaps the most astounding thing about this piece of work was its distinctiveness from any other detergents advertising that had gone before. We had moved from the confines of the kitchen and the washing room to the freedom of the beach. We had gone outside, away from the contrived hysterical world of stains, problems and hopelessness into the real timeless world of possibility and hope.

But rather than bombard our consumers with fact after spurious fact, in the marathon voiceover that would normally be squeezed into 30 seconds of marketing thuggery – we had embraced much more the power of silence. For we had realised that the way we would create true empathy was by listening. And to listen you have to stop speaking.

By creating such periods of silence in the words of this one-minute epic, we were providing space for the insight to connect and land with those watching. The airing of the words, the inflection of the voiceover and the huge periods of natural silence which would surround it would ease the consumer into this new empathetic world. As the camera lifted to reveal the splendour of the whale, so too would the very paradox that 'dirt can be a good thing' be revealed to those watching on their TV screens.

We had engaged with the Brazilian, Indian, French, Turkish and American housewives with a series of unfinished sentences. And by leaving the sentence unfinished we were inviting our consumers to share in our understanding of their dreams. Stimulus was to make a very virtuous circle of our consumers' responses.

Paradoxically, by hearing what wasn't being said, they were to connect with our new take on the world and the role of our

69

brand within it.

It was to prove one of the most powerful pieces of advertising the company had ever seen, being shown across four continents with massive consumer responsiveness wherever it went. For those in need of quantitative hard-data to underscore its success, it provided in abundance.

Our brands had spent years fixating on information which was all too often spurious and usually boring. We had finally managed to break this habit, focussing instead on making a real emotional connection with the dreams and aspirations of every woman and man on earth.

But the achievement was bigger than that of simply making a good film. We had finally started to disprove the rationalists who had struggled with what they perceived to be a lack of 'functionality' within the 'Dirt is Good' thinking.

'Beach Art' was to show and prove that by connecting with our consumers' dreams in such a profound way, we were effectively proving an undying devotion to their every need. And the fact that we would perform immaculately in the cleaning challenge was one assumed by parents. How else could a brand have the audacity to know so clearly what its consumers were dreaming if it could not be trusted unconditionally to clean?

Our destination could not have been more different from the place of embarkation. Far from the natural rugged beauty of the beach where dirtiness and freedom basked in unselfconscious harmony, we would gather in the über-chic minimalism of Miami's Delano hotel. We were surrounded by minimalist whiteness and sterility interrupted only by the occasional fake-tan. The freedom of the natural Brazilian mountainscape replaced with the silicon perfection of the über-chic. It could not have been a more contrasting world from the one we were starting to access in our consumers' dreams.

For the first time ever the various fiefdoms of the global

advertising network had gathered in one and the same place in an unprecedented congregation of egos and super-egos. It was not by accident that all of this creative talent sat together as one in the backyard of our biggest competitor.

We had approached this briefing with the kind of draconian rigour we had imposed on the consumer mining exploration. Loved by globalists and loathed by much of the rest of the world, we had created a single global brief. We had erased many of the lines which had so artificially carved up our consumers. We would now go one step further by levelling the world's best creative talent behind one and the same mountainous brief.

How could it be that we would continue to be divided in our intentions by the mere fact that our advertising network had spawned tens of offices through the years and hundreds of egos to fill them?

We figured that if only all of this talent could work together in rigorous co-operation, as opposed to competitive isolation, we might stand a chance of cracking this gargantuan brief.

We were asking this collection of 28 creative teams to overturn the convention which had infested advertising reels the world over. The convention that dirty kids equals bad mothers. We were asking our talent to 'make mothers feel good about kids getting dirty'. In other words, we were to assert that 'good mothers are the ones that let their kids get dirty'.

We wanted a creative idea which could reconcile the conflict between freedom and authority.

And in line with this we were to give them the freedom of a tight brief with an even tighter reporting regime. Every Thursday for a period of five weeks each office would submit their work to a single global creative leader for feedback by the end of the week.

We had finally imposed order on the free thinkers and they were beginning to almost enjoy it.

71

Gathering for cocktails around the perfectly straight edges of the sleek infinity pool, we looked out to the ocean.

The sea was beginning to swell.

Lessons

1 The freedom of a tight brief.

By bringing together the global creative community behind a single common brief, we had already broken convention. Further, the brief had been meticulously refined through the previous iterations and learnings – and had the confidence to ask of 28 teams to bring to life a single thought: 'The freedom to get dirty'. We continued to resist the temptation to slip in some of the conventional discourse about functionality – leaving this very much assumed in the bigger thought.

2 Set the brand world in humanity at large.

Having followed a meticulous process to elevate the brand's perspective beyond the category conventions, and into the real life and dreams of our consumer, it follows that the creative territory should be such a timeless idyll. The beach setting was to prove a powerful symbol of the freedom pathway that our brand would now walk.

3 Create a virtuoso performance.

'Beach Art' was to prove that we were speaking differently about the category – and showing that the brand has a different view on the world. This was represented in the minute-long time length of the film, the minimalism of voiceover and the total absence of all of the standard points of reference for a detergent ad.

Circus

Creating brand believers globally. In which we set about 'stewarding' the brand across the world so that all internal players have a common and inspiring understanding of the brand.

There was something tragic about the figure of the clown, sitting exhausted outside the big tent, head in hands and make-up smudged, surrounded by the idyllic beauty of Maresias. Thrown on the beach by his side was his bag, on which was emblazoned a large red cross.

He was no ordinary clown, for in fact he was a 'happiness doctor'. For his day job he would travel around hospitals of Brazil visiting sick children – often terminally ill – with the aim of making them laugh. A clown dressed as a doctor using medical paraphernalia to create comedy for children with little to laugh about.

Connecting emotionally with people when the physical and functional is under duress.

But this was not his day job. He had been invited, along with about 100 others, to the first ever 'Dirt is Good' brand experience event.

We had battled over the last three years to ensure that the senior players were working with, as opposed to against, the team. More than once we had found ourselves surging forward into attack with our idea only to be thwarted by a surreptitious side-tackle by our own players. The idea was declared too soft, too hard or just too not invented here. We had learnt, through bitter experience, the need to keep all players on side with our thinking. We had also learnt that no matter how much we had tried to change the minds of those convinced our idea was wrong, the more the sounds of protest would become unbearably shrill. We were reminded of the immortal words of a former leader: 'You can't teach a pig to sing. It sounds bad and irritates the pig'.

The opportunity now was to get deep into the businesses and the areas of functional expertise who could make this idea really come alive in the marketplace. Come alive in the lives of the women the world over who had responded so positively as we tapped into the latent insight that 'Dirt is Good'.

Six months would pass as we meticulously dissected our internal audience throughout the company into different target groups, defining as we went increasingly tight objectives for this event. We would pinpoint the obstacles to understanding the brand region-by-region in order that we might address them one-by-one in our approach.

We would base our brand experience event on the mission our core brand team had recently coined as the brand's rallying cry: 'To allow people to live, love and experience the "Dirt is Good" idea'. It seemed apposite that those sitting on the corporate side of the mirror should share in exactly the same conversion to 'Dirt is Good' as we were asking consumers to do beyond the mirror.

Over a two-day event – to be repeated across four continents – we would invite people on the journey to 'Dirt is Good'. We would immerse them in the experiences and learning that the brand team itself had experienced. And as the brand idea emerged, so too would the environment, in which the event was held, change to reflect this.

As we walk into the big tent on the beach front between Sao Paulo and Rio de Janeiro, we are confronted by an amazing sense of total whiteness. For all around is the totally blank canvas of a pristine world – as yet unlived-in and undirtied by those undergoing the brand immersion experience. All around is total pristine clean.

In sympathy with their totally clean environment, all of the potential brand converts are dressed in simple, uniform white. Totally clean, totally uniform. Momentary flashbacks to some far-away lunatic asylum blacken the mind for an instant.

And as we immerse ourselves in the conception of the 'Dirt is Good' idea, as we discover the true force of dirt, our environment starts to move us. And to move itself.

For the clinical sterility and coldness becomes alive with the vivid dashes of paint which fill the walls and spill onto the floors. The institutionalised white of the uniforms is gradually transformed to different shades of dirtiness.

We see the face of a hitherto straight-laced technical manager gripped by concentration as he paints the most brilliant of masterpieces, brought to life with a shocking array of gay colours. The inner world is slowly coming out onto the safer confines of the canvas which confronts him.

We see the wanton abandon as dirt and mud, food and drink are allowed to fly through the air. We see the simple joy that clay, water and creative hands can bring to the most reserved of managers.

The clinically white asylum-like tent transforms over two days into a thoroughly lived-in temple of creativity, dirt and achievement. Getting dirty has driven this transformation.

As day one unfolds we will explore what it really means to connect emotionally with human beings. We will see tears of laughter and sorrow in the audience as the 'happiness doctors' tell their story of human connection and emotion. It is a metaphor for what we need our brand to do. It is fascinating that the 'happiness doctors' evoke the same response and have similar stories to tell in every continent. Their currency of emotional connection does not seem to be at all denominated by nationality.

We will hear from child psychologists and play experts who will enjoin the usually reserved corporate audience in the wild and frenetic dirty play of children.

We will explore the world of the brands we love – Nike, Apple, Levi's. And we will bring the new initiates into the vivid brand world, a world our team has so loved to explore over the years of creating the 'Dirt is Good' brand idea.

Steve Jobs will tell us about the Apple brand as if he is in the room with us.

And we will talk about achievement. What it really means – from the perspective of Latin parents to those that modern Asian parents have for their children. We will see emerge a richness around the insight and the brand idea, which is deepened by the discussions which are being provoked. We will tease out the difference which exists in how Northern European mothers see the challenge of parenting versus their

Southern European counterparts, only to decide that the difference isn't quite as big as we first believed.

The roller-coaster ride of day one will then lead – our audience now very dirty – into a day two experience designed to understand the mechanics of the brand. The 'Splat'; the advertising strategy; innovation; PR.

We will end the day with a task to test whether the newly initiated are breathing 'Dirt is Good' in their souls. For we will give each team the task of creating a new TV spot that celebrates the 'Dirt is Good' idea with the world outside. Armed with little more than a hand-held camera, a naturally dirty environment and a new fervour for the brand, the teams are to create the most engaging and hilarious ideas that even the worst advertising networks would struggle to surpass.

We will line up all initiates against the now dirty walls, covered in creativity, in order of their degree of buy-in, nay devotion to the brand idea. And we will hear the impassioned plea of the most fervent of the new mujahedeen, as he declares dirty war on any of the infidels remaining in Europe.

And as we finally hit the crescendo of our two days' brand initiation experience, we are to break out from the tent into the freedom of the beach.

Here we have constructed the world's biggest mud bath in a kind of inflatable swimming pool the size of a football pitch. Swilling with dirt and paint, mud and water and 100 human bodies, we will see the world's dirtiest and most exhilarating game of 'Splatball' ever. A game we have designed to bring out the ingenious, creative and sheer dirty in all concerned.

The two days will end with a mass of human bodies covered from head to toe in dirt and mud, wallowing on the beach. Even the most senior and most reserved of converts is seen to be enjoined in this orgy of dirt.

★ ★ ★

The clown picked up his medical bag and walked off into the sunset, leaving the clamour of the masses behind.

It sure was a strange world. And for a moment he could have sworn he could hear a pig singing.

Lessons

1 Create a powerful brand experience for internal teams so that they can *feel* the idea.

We went to extraordinary effort to bring the 'Dirt is Good' idea to life for all of the internal audiences across the world. This was to be a huge investment both in time and money – but one which was undoubtedly worth it. Central to the whole experiential design of the stewardship events was the tremendous sense of experience. By being invited to truly feel the idea, and to experience the liberation of getting dirty first hand, individuals and teams could embody the idea fully.

2 Aim for brand zealots, not just brand acceptors.

We used the brand stewardship sessions to extract a personal commitment from all the players necessary for the brand's success henceforth. By forcing this level of personal engagement, we would see a remarkable level of subsequent commitment to the brand's success.

Sunlight

Delivering brand conceived innovation.
In which we come to terms with the need for brand conceived innovation – ie innovation driven through the lens of the brand.

High above the clouds in the Bolivian mountains above La Paz, where man dare not go, the most extraordinary sight comes into view. Away from the day-to-day concerns of everyday folk, the most bizarre of scenes was there for all not to see.

For here at the top of the mountain was row upon row upon row of washing, hanging in the most perfect arrangement of lines, all of which joined in a gargantuan, post-modern maze that somehow had neither beginning nor end.

In amongst this seemingly interminable washday nightmare were the white coats of what appeared to be scientists, somehow locked in this giant laundry labyrinth.

They looked up at the fierce sunlight as if somehow assessing its natural wonder, as its merciless rays seemed to brand the rows of shirts like a red hot poker.

Although it was maybe just an illusion that the extremes of nature can make appear real, it did seem that the washing was somehow changing in front of their very eyes. For what seemed at first to be freshly clean garments were strangely – upon closer examination – still dirty. Fresh, clean, dirty laundry. But as the sun insisted in its mission it was as if the stains which had remained on the freshly hung out laundry were disappearing.

But this was not some hallucination, for the scientists seemed to take this miracle very much in their purposeful strides as they marched ever more proudly around the maze-like rows of laundry, inspecting their subjects standing starch-stiff to attention in front of them.

The young boy ascended the mountain from the plain below. He surveyed this most extraordinary of scenes from his make-believe telescope. He had some vague notion of what a scientist or at least an inventor might be. It had been the dream of his friends and his family to grow up to be something as exciting as an inventor. But he had not expected them to look quite like this nor to be locked in this bizarre maze of laundry hanging out dirty in the blazing Bolivian sun.

Suddenly he heard their voices come together in what seemed like alarm as they grabbed hold of one of the garments and inspected what for an awful moment appeared to be a hole – burned into the fabric of the garment by the fierce Andean sun. But he could not understand their words and cursing – seeming to him like some kind of corporate double dutch or what he imagined Irish might sound like.

Bewildered but intrigued, he stuffed his makeshift telescope into his pocket and fled the scene of the miraculous maze for the mundane safety of his mother down below.

And as he arrived home and told his tall tale, he was greeted by the disinterested humouring that busy mums give to young boys with over-active imaginations when they are too busy to entertain their childish fantasies. The toil of wash day was hard enough – slaving at the edge of the river and using one's whole body to scrub away the dirt – without endless fantasies and talk of bizarre inventors and their mountain top experiments.

Though the scientists could think these ideas, they were not in any real way related to the world of the consumer. A world of dirt being good. In short it was a case of what could be made, as opposed to innovation conceived through the lens of the brand idea. Innovation as the means by which consumers experience the idea palpably.

Back in Brazil the team had gathered to think about invention and innovation in the very real context of the newly coined 'Dirt is Good' brand.

And for the very first time it was now possible to think of innovation in a joined up way – joined up by the universal power of the brand insight and its discriminating proposition to the world of washing. It offered parents and their children

85

the 'freedom to get dirty'.

It seemed to the team that there was a dissonance with the way these brands had innovated in years gone by and how it now seemed appropriate to channel all innovation through this single brand idea called 'Dirt is Good'. For rather than appear 'breakthrough', 'revolutionary' or even just 'new' the spurious 'technical improvements' which would appear with tedious regularity from the laboratories in years gone by now seemed somehow tired and disconnected.

The team was becoming restless. It would remark that if all of these 'innovations' were really so innovative then how come both ourselves and our competitors were witnessing the slow erosion of global market share by cheaper, less innovative competitors?

The challenge would be to take the idea of 'Dirt is Good' and to conceive of news which would truly engage real people through the lens of the brand idea, as opposed to through the microscopic lens of the laboratory.

The organising thought started to emerge: 'Dirt is Good. It's cleaning that is bad'.

Rather than proclaiming our new efficacy by protesting too much about the size of our molecules, we could stimulate a positive impression of performance by engaging consumers in a truly intimate conversation about their lives. But how?

The team went back into the reams of reports that accompanied the original insight mining from which 'Modern Parenting' and latterly 'Dirt is Good' had been excavated. Surely hidden in this mine of information was the clue to a truly brand-conceived approach.

And here sandwiched between the pages of a research report we see again the timeless images we have used to uncover the rich vein of thinking that has become "Dirt is Good". Here is young Picasso accompanied by the caption which invites consumers to 'let kids express themselves and let their creativity grow'.

Here is a young boy kicking around a muddy football dreaming of one day becoming Ronaldinho. And as we read the line 'every great footballer began by kicking a muddy ball around a yard' it seems somehow a million miles more interesting than the diet of molecules and false technology hyperbolised out of all meaningful proportion and disconnected from the real world of consumers which we feel we now understand.

But it's the image of the child stuffing his make-believe tools into his pocket as he surveys his newly assembled go-cart that inspires us. Accompanied by the caption 'great engineers start young' the image strikes a chord.

Isn't it true that in the very confines of these and other children's pockets the world over lie the pieces of a child's boundless imagination? Isn't it true for children the world over that their pockets are the secret store of all their inventive and creative dreams?

And isn't it true that by looking inside these pockets, grubby and filthy, with tens of hands having gone in and out of them as the day's intriguing adventures unfold, that we see something altogether wondrous?

We would conceive of the pocket as the theatre of children's dreams, hopes and aspirations, observed not through the lens of the microscope but with the vicarious pride of their mums looking on.

'Kids explore the world with their hands – hands which collect the dirtiest of treasures and are then shoved into their pockets'.

We enter the dirty world of children through the brand insight, celebrating children's freedom to get dirty and, therefore, guaranteeing perfect results first time. We would guarantee perfect results by leaving the clear impression that we could clean the dirtiest insides of pockets which have held their dirty treasures. We were both showing how dirt can be good, and proving how we alleviated the chore of the washday.

There was indeed some chemistry – albeit quite modest – involved in delivering this notion. But, rather than obsess about this, instead we engage via the brand. For once our innovation starts to seem natural – born from the brand as opposed to being imposed irrelevantly upon it.

But rather than being just an announcement of news, the pockets theme is to inspire a whole programme of engaging activity which will surround the consumer at every touchpoint and interaction with the brand. Our consumer sees from every angle how intriguing the unassuming world of children's pockets can be.

Advertising will dramatise the relatively modest dirty articles hidden in a child's pockets and project forward into what might be the signal of a child's future. Hence pockets containing grass and plants would signal 'Joao – future biologist'.

The dusty bones unearthed and stuffed into another child's pocket will conjure up 'Luca – future archaeologist'.

A dirty twig used to poke at a makeshift go-cart will signal a budding 'future mechanic'.

And the 'Pockets' advertising will be shot and shown across five continents – the idea and script remaining true to the original, almost to the word. The only difference nation-to-nation will be the casting and the voiceover.

From being hopelessly local we have become mindfully global.

The advertising will go on to score higher than any innovation advertising that has gone before and all of this without mindlessly flaunting our molecules.

But it's beyond the advertising that it really comes alive. The Brazilian team goes on to develop a consistent brand-inspired theme which brings the pockets idea into vivid technicolour reality.

In Brazil alone the target of hitting 10 million people directly and 40 million people indirectly is reached through the seemingly unprepossessing prism of the pocket.

'Pockets full of talent and no stains' will inspire parents and children throughout Brazil, Turkey, Morocco, Thailand, Indonesia, Spain, France, India, South Africa and many other nations. A school bus will be decorated as a temple of potential – emblazoned with pockets. Mass events are convened outside of supermarkets with activities inside of giant pockets. Indeed pockets will become the rallying cry of brand activation the world over in the first global roll out of a single innovation project.

From a previous time of some 780 projects, all of which had minimal impact and maximum fragmentation, just one simple idea would unite innovation, sales forces, marketing teams as well as consumers behind this simple expression of the brand.

The boy pulled his makeshift telescope from his pocket and looked up at the top of the mountain beyond the clouds. But the strange rows of laundry, blowing rigidly in the wind, had miraculously dissolved.

Lessons

1 Use the brand idea as the lens for brand conceived innovation.

The Brand Idea should act as the lens for sifting innovation – such that when the brand does innovate it is congruent with the Brand Idea – and touches the motivating insight which sits behind the brand's power to motivate.

We were to learn that a whole host of innovation that had not been conceived this way round would prove ultimately unusable. Technology – however clever, was not relevant to the idea or the consumer – would not pass muster. Conversely, by starting to integrate the idea into thinking, we could remould technologies that existed already to fit the brand idea. It was this that led to 'Pockets' as an interpretation of what was in fact modest technology.

2 Use this to drive connection across every touch point.

When conceived through the lens of the brand, innovation has the power to truly communicate across multiple touchpoints, whilst saying cumulatively one and the same thing. The 'Pockets' idea was the very first exemplar of this.

3 By changing the category definition – via the Brand Idea – we open up totally new opportunities for innovation.

We were to shift the category definition – short-handed as 'Dirt is good, it's cleaning that's bad!' This fundamentally bigger, yet tighter brief would inspire an innovation funnel which would later include 'Splatwear'– a range of 'dirt friendly' clothing which was easy to clean.

Movement

Spreading the word
via brand activism
and activation.
In which we mobilise
consumers the world
over through the power
of the brand idea... and
see the world finally
become one.

He was an unlikely source of inspiration. Dishevelled and somehow managing to maintain an air of being permanently dirty, Bob Geldof was not the archetypal front man for a gathering, the ostensible purpose of which was to make the world's clothes cleaner.

He had become more than a passing symbol of hope for the great unwashed, the masses who, were it not for him, would have remained utterly indifferent to the human plight which, only 20 years ago, was set to rip Africa apart and unleash global disaster.

And as we gathered in the spartan simplicity of the Soweto Zebra Lodge, there was something particularly apposite about Geldof being there. He brought an almost palpable freedom of spirit, which leapt out from the television screen in front of us and punched us in the face. And as he swore and ranted, he inflamed in us a contagious and blistering passion which jumped around the room between us in much the same way that sparks jump from a fire long after the prodding has stopped and the poker has been laid down.

He was speaking about his own personal mission to bring survival and dignity to those who had been starving in the North East of where we were now sitting – some 20 years ago. But strangely the messages he conveyed were more than pertinent for us today as we contemplated how to mobilise the world behind the idea of 'Dirt is Good'. His very words took on an almost unreal relevance for us.

'You can't harness wishy washiness,' he almost spat into the screen. 'You need to give people a membership card to get them actively engaging in what you are trying to achieve.'

As we listened in captivated silence, an inaudible applause would rise up in each of us to greet his every word, like the 'ole's' which greet the every flourish of a passionate bull-fighter as he stalks his prey.

'I wanted it not to be a passive experience, I wanted it to be active,' he continued. 'I wanted people to be mobilised behind something they did care about and I soon realised that the lingua franca of the world was not English, it was actually pop music.'

Geldof went on to create the biggest shared experience in human history, with a third of the human race watching the Live Aid event and raising via one record more money than the total annual Unicef budget for Africa.

But it was his follow-up event which had even greater pertinence. He was to create the biggest sports event ever. And as Geldof shouted 'Change the world!', 20 million people took part in the biggest symbolic joining of hands across 77 countries in 277 cities as they took to the streets to run in the name of 'Run the World'.

We were stunned by the scale of his achievement and felt that it related with incredible purpose to our very own cause. We had gathered some weeks prior to this in Sao Paulo to look at how our brand had been activating the 'Dirt is Good' idea to date. And though results had been impressive we wanted to realise a different scale of mobilisation.

We had started to understand that if we were to shift market share we would have to motivate people – move people to act differently – to move their behaviours in the name of our 'Dirt is Good' idea. And with a simple jump in logic we understood that the way in which we could recruit people into our brand was to get them dirty. Their membership card was dirt.

Suddenly it felt like a much clearer rallying cry than the sterile business-speak of old. 'How could we get half of the world to get dirty?' If we could make people just half militant about this idea we could make them act in the name of our brand. And if they acted in the name of our brand then our share would move.

In some ways Pakistan – a conservative Islamic country in which cleanliness is next to something like godliness – might not seem the most likely place for the 'Dirt is Good' brand to bring mass entertainment to the streets in what was the biggest marketing event the country had ever seen. But to limit expectations merely due to the cultural heritage of the country would be an injustice to the energy and commitment that the team would bring to bear in the name of 'Dirt is Good'.

Armed only with the fervent conviction that Pakistan as much as, if not more than, other countries would respond to the insight that getting dirty can be a good thing, the team got to work. It was to spend the next three months working every weekend, staying in the most insalubrious places in the hinterland of Pakistan, taking neither weekends nor holidays.

The Surf brand had been assaulted by the launch of Ariel as the Cincinnati monster lengthened its reach in the backwaters of Central Asia. Slowly but surely the brand had been diminished by a superior product backed by a media spend some five times that of Surf. Within months it had generated awareness of 54% with a brand recall of 96%. And this was to translate into a market share of 13% by the end of the year. There was every sense in the team that a landslide was to start out of hard soaps and into a newly energised powders sector led by Ariel.

The task before the team was to translate the success it had seen for 'Dirt is Good' in visits to Latin America and North Africa and bring this to the proletariat of Pakistan.

The team had already launched the 'Modern Parenting' communication – showing in simple terms that by getting dirty, children would learn good life skills. This had been brought to life in events around the big cities which highlighted children's achievements accomplished whilst getting dirty.

But it was not until 2003 that the Surf brand really

brought 'Dirt is Good' to the masses by an event called Paint Masti. The team had been planning this for some six months. Rather than trying to beat Ariel head on at its own game, it would beat it by a relevant and tangible approach to 'Dirt is Good' which connected people with the latent and motivational needs of the Pakistani people at large. Paint Masti was to become an event which would get the children of Pakistan painting across 110 towns and 600,000 consumers. The team would travel across the country for three months making this happen.

By purchasing a packet of Surf a family gained entry to the Paint Masti event, which was pre-marketed by national and local artists and prominent educationalists. They extolled the merits of painting in developing children's creativity and urged participation.

Each day a new set of people would attend the mass-painting event and this would then be televised in order to keep awareness and momentum high. PR would ensure maximum awareness. For the duration of this huge campaign, the Surf team refused to resort to price cuts and incentivisation of the trade. The team figured that the brand message, and the consequent consumer pull it would generate, would prove incentivisation enough.

The brand gained three share points over the period at the direct expense of Ariel. Brand margins were more than doubled. Brand attributes shifted radically to the positive at the competitor's expense. We had made an almost overnight mass conversion of the population into the brand via their experience of the idea.

The Pakistani Chairman smiled as she heard the Head of Police for Karachi municipality yelling down the phone: "Too many bloody people. Too many bloodyfucking people an all!" He shook his head affirmatively in disbelief. Paint Masti had blocked the main arterial road of Karachi as hoards of wannabe artists and their parents headed for the event.

Geldof would have been proud.

In Brazil the team wanted to go further. Its ambition was to make 14,000,000 people – that is 50% of households – tangibly living the 'Dirt is Good' idea. Like Geldof before them the team had recognised the vast potential of sport as a mass medium for engagement.

The whole of the brand world, from every continent, had gathered in Sao Paulo to discuss sport and its direct relevance to bringing 'Dirt is Good' alive. We realised that not only was sport absolutely synonymous with the values of our brand, but it also made consumers actually act on the 'Dirt is Good' idea. And by acting in this way they would be actually putting a part of themselves into the brand experience. The brand was to get the whole of the world living 'Dirt is Good' via the lens of sport.

We had consulted with the top sports psychologists, motivationalists and child psychologists. A 'white paper' had been published by a fast-becoming famous child psychologist called Dr John Richer. Prior to this commission some said he was simply known as Dr John Rich. He had been commissioned to explain with scientific evidence the virtues of sport and getting dirty in a child's development.

We were ready to go. Brazil would lead the charge.

★ ★ ★

The starting point was to announce the linkage between sport and the brand – by establishing the thought that without dirt there would be no sport and without sport there would be no learning. We were playing in a huge arena – the arena of sport – but we brought to it a unique new relevance via the perspective of getting dirty. 'Marks and Signs' was shot by the same director as 'Beach Art'. It showed that if you did not get dirty when doing sport, then the sport itself was no longer of any value. It was a total discontinuity from the hysterical advertising predecessors of stains gone mad.

Next we would bring home Brazil's national hero Ronaldinho to sponsor our initiative. We would invite families to attend massive events at which Ronaldinho himself would appear. The focus of the event would be on teaching life skills through sport – and in the process of this – getting dirty.

With learnings from Pakistan the events were to be massively pre-marketed and then reported post-event in the news. As part of the event we would create our very own game called 'Splatball' – a team game in which participants would play a new kind of football but would be rewarded for managing to get their team dirty by means of a massive rubber 'Splat'.

At store level we were to offer a colossal national promotion in which consumers could redeem pack-top tokens for a miniature collectable 'Splatball'. This would cause a phenomenon across the retail landscape of Brazil. People would queue for hours to redeem their tokens and finally get their hands on the coveted balls. 'Splatmania' was launched.

But the activity was not merely commercial. We would go on to plan the building of new arenas in the wastelands of the favelas – working alongside Brazil's foremost humanitarian charities.

In other parts of the world, in the months and years that follow, new variations spring to life in different cultures. All take their inspiration from the single idea that has galvanised us as a team. 'Dirt is Good' has become our mantra and our guiding light.

So, other countries in Latin and North America, in Africa

and Asia, started to explore the idea through nature, art and sport. Ideas of improvisation and freedom clustered around exemplars like Ronaldinho and the painter Homero Brito. Asian parents – in Thailand, India, Vietnam and Indonesia – were persuaded that getting dirty could deliver a greater measure of freedom. But the persuasion was gentle, it was no big task, because the idea seems inherent in all of us, wherever we are. South Africa, emerging from the apartheid years, launched an art challenge that engaged thousands of parents and children. The link between dirt and a child's development was made.

And in Turkey, 'Dirt is Good' arrived during economic crisis and price wars, against a backdrop of belief that dirt is anti-Islamic. So a big debate was begun among opinion leaders through the media. Psychiatrists and child development experts proclaimed the virtues of dirt while new advertising set out our beliefs: 'You can't live by observing life through a window. You can't do things without getting dirty'. Then sports festivals in eight cities brought together our philosophy with the consumers' philosophy, as one. Consumers – mothers, fathers, children – became our spokespeople, and they all proclaimed 'Dirt is Good'.

There is a thunderous clatter as three helicopters arrive somehow on the horizon, parting the glow of the African sky with the darting urgency of machines.

And like the leopards below which roam the Soweto plain, the helicopters make a sudden last-ditch run at their prey. Creeping up slowly and furtively only to then pounce on the earth in an instant – parting the bone dry grass in their wake – to where we stand.

And the thundering noise of the clattering blades somehow confers a frozen silence around us as we run beneath the whirring blades and scramble on board.

Suddenly and effortlessly we lift high above the desiccated plain, the helicopter knifing the still of the African sky as if shaking it awake and into action.

And down below we see the slightly blurred shapes of the fields and the burning haze of the sun starting to merge into one. The harsh lines of irrigation with which they are divided start to merge into a seamless patchwork of space and potential.

As different animals start to appear as distinct and different shapes below us, they are nonetheless somehow united as one in our new aerial view.

And we see the zebras below – the black and white of their stripes somehow merging as if someone has erased the lines without smudging the colours.

It is as if the world has merged into one.

Lessons

1 Create Brand Activists and Brand Activism in the name of the Brand Idea.

We were to create teams of what we would call 'brand mujahedeen'– believers who would now take the responsibility of spreading the brand via activation programmes across the most remote and populous parts of the world.

The 'Painting' activity, and later 'Sport' are good examples of brand activation which is truly brand conceived, hence truly distinctive – yet surprisingly easy to activate regardless of stage of market development.

2 Use emerging markets as the agents of change – and create audacious and exciting common goals.

It was ultimately many of the much smaller markets which would build real traction for the 'Dirt is Good' idea across the world. The hunger for change, and the relative cheapness of media, proved a useful backdrop for the idea reaching the less obvious corners of the world.

Equally important was a sense of the scale of ambition – a desire to think and act big in all that the brand would do. Hence we spoke of 'getting half the world dirty' as part of our activation programme – inspired by the experience of Live Aid.

3 Understand the world as one.

By seeing the world as one, and persistently building approaches to the brand's creation and execution which were truly joined up, the power of scale and mutual learning was to be opened up infinitely.

About the author

David Arkwright is the founding partner of MEAT – a global brand development agency which works with brands the world over, to create transformative big brand ideas.

Prior to this he led the creation of 'Dirt is Good' – an idea which has transformed Unilever's laundry business.

MEAT was formed in 2005 by David Arkwright and Katie Oakley to help businesses and brand owners to build global brands which connect at a fundamental human level. Prior to forming MEAT, David spent five years as Global VP, responsible for Unilever's top performance laundry business globally – resulting in 'Dirt is Good' as a unifying global idea. Katie was Managing Director of Henley Centre Headlight Vision where she helped many big brands to navigate the challenges of the future via deeper, better insight, working latterly on 'Dirt is Good'.

MEAT works with brands the world over to create globally compelling brand ideas. Clients include GSK, Bacardi, BP, SAB Miller and Unilever.